BETHLEHEM

An Advent Journey

David W. Graybeal

Parson's Porch Books

BETHLEHEM

An Advent Journey

Acknowledgements

There are several people who have inspired, influenced, and informed my own journey in bringing this book to birth. First of all, as I indicate in the dedication, I am grateful for my mom, Anne Graybeal, who first introduced me to the stories and songs of Bethlehem in our family home during my earliest Advents as a child. Her abiding faith in Christ and her abounding love for others continue to inspire me even after she has joined the communion of saints.

I am grateful for the company with whom my wife Tracy and I traveled to the Holy Land in the spring of 2014, Educational Opportunities Tours, and our guides, Saad and Mike, for their introducing us to the places and the peoples of this sacred ground. I am especially grateful for our fellow pilgrims from the church where I was serving at the time—Larry and Bonnie Mauldin, and Fred and Liz McBee—for accompanying us on this journey that "keeps on giving" and continues to generate reflection.

I am grateful for the congregation with whom this material was first shared, where it originated as an Advent sermon series in 2014—St. Mark United Methodist Church in Knoxville, Tennessee—as well as the congregation where I revisited these reflections in

2023—Signal Crest United Methodist Church in Signal Mountain, Tennessee.

I am grateful for friends and colleagues who have offered encouragement to me in this project and read drafts of this material and offered comments, suggestions, and even endorsements: Claire Brown, Brad Hyde, Andrew Lay, Peter Miano, Lyn Pace, Don Saliers, Will Shelton, and Bill Thornton. I am also grateful for David Tullock, publisher at Parson's Porch Books, for his support of this project and his guidance throughout the publishing process.

Finally, I am grateful for my wife Tracy with whom I shared this journey to the Holy Land and with whom I share the journey of marriage, ministry, and parenthood, and to our two sons Noah and Wesley, in whom my soul takes such joy and delight.

And I am grateful for you, the reader of this book, for your sharing in this Advent journey. I pray that it will be a blessing to you and will draw you nearer to the heart of the unfathomable mystery of the incarnation of God in the life, the ministry, the death, and the resurrection of the one born a long time ago in the little town of Bethlehem.

This book is dedicated in memory of my
mother

Anne Graybeal (1931–2023)

who first introduced me to Bethlehem

in story and song.

Contents

An Invitation to Bethlehem 11

First Sunday of Advent 22
   Hope

A Mother's Voice from Bethlehem 24
   Genesis 35:16–20

Second Sunday of Advent 40
   Love

A Redeemer in Bethlehem 42
   Ruth 4:7–12

Third Sunday of Advent 55
   Joy

A New King in Bethlehem 57
   1 Samuel 16:1–13

Fourth Sunday of Advent 70
   Peace

A Vision for Peace in Bethlehem 72
   Micah 5:2–5

Christmas Eve 88
   Christ

Let Us Go Now to Bethlehem 90
   Luke 2:1–20

Bibliography 105

An Invitation to Bethlehem

Bethlehem.

The name itself is shrouded in mystery. No one seems to be sure what it actually means. It may come from the Canaanite *Beit Lamhi,* "House of Lahmi," referring to one of the ancient local gods of that region. It also might mean *Beit Lechem,* which means "House of Bread." But its rolling hills seem less suited for grain than for grazing. So its Arabic name *Beit Lahm,* "House of Meat," might be more fitting. It also may be related to the Aramaic language that Jesus spoke, *Beit Lamra,* "House of Lamb," which makes sense if there were indeed shepherds keeping watch over their flocks there, as the scripture says in Luke 2.[1] So which is it? House of Bread, or House of Meat, or House of Lamb? We don't really know.

But just hearing the name can conjure various images in our mind's eyes.

One of my earliest encounters with the name Bethlehem came when I was a very young child. Every Advent, my mom would bring out our family's nativity set and set it on top of the piano in our living room. It was a simple wooden structure with flaky green paper

---

[1] Blincoe, *Bethlehem,* 6–8.

shreds loosely glued onto the roof and little strands of straw strewn about the floor.

At some point in December, usually as we were getting closer to Christmas, she would call my brother and me together and read to us the Christmas story from the Gospel accounts, from Luke 2 and then from Matthew 2. We would take the figurines for Mary and Joseph into our small hands, and we would lead them across the green carpet and over our sand-colored couch to represent their long journey from Nazareth in Galilee to the city of David called Bethlehem in Judea. We would then place them behind the manger, with serene Mary kneeling cribside in her soft blue shawl and protective Joseph standing watch beside her in his dark red robe.

When it came time in the story for Mary to deliver her child and lay him in the manger, we would gently place the mid-squirm baby Jesus in his swaddling clothes in a bedful of hay. And when it came time for the shepherds to appear upon the announcement of the angel of the Lord, we would arrange the curious shepherds with their smattering of sheep along the margins of the manger and the angel atop it all in its glistening gold and white robe with gossamer wings. And then when it came time in the story for the magi to appear guided by the star, we would parade them in from the next room (because it said they came from afar) and we'd place the three majestic figures with their camels and their crowns and their colorful robes and their exotic gifts.

Finally, when everyone was in their proper place, mom would sit down at the piano and lead us in singing Christmas carols. Some of my favorites were "Away in a Manger," "Joy to the World," "Silent Night," and, of course, "O Little Town of Bethlehem." I grew up in a small town in southwestern Virginia, so I could easily imagine that the Savior of the world was born in a sleepy little town like ours, where the stars passed silently in the sky even as the trucks passed more noisily by on the interstate.

Since then, however, different images of Bethlehem have come to mingle in my mind alongside these early memories.

No Little Town of Bethlehem

In the spring of 2014, some members of the church I was serving accompanied my wife Tracy and me on a pilgrimage to the Holy Land. We took the so-called "classic tour" which included several of the major sites in the scriptures and especially in the story of Jesus. We visited his hometown of Nazareth and Cana where he turned the water into wine at the wedding reception (John 2:1–11). We visited the ruins of Capernaum where he called the fishermen to follow him and the

Sea of Galilee where he calmed the storm and walked on water. We visited a potential site of his baptism by John in the Jordan River near the mouth of the Dead Sea (where we floated and caked our faces with mud). And we visited several sites in and around Jerusalem, including the Western Wall, the Mount of Olives, the Garden of Gethsemane, the house of the high priest Caiaphas and Herod's fortress, the Upper Room, the Church of the Holy Sepulcher, and the so-called "Garden Tomb." And, of course, we visited Bethlehem.

I discovered that Bethlehem is not so little of a town any longer. It's a busy, bustling city that has become a suburb of Jerusalem. The only way you know you've left one and entered the other is when you pass through the graffiti-covered concrete barrier wall that separates Bethlehem in the Palestinian territory of the West Bank (of the Jordan River) from Israeli territory. Bethlehem's narrow streets and passageways are lined with shops and markets where tourists can purchase all kinds of handcrafted items, spices, and olive wood carvings. We stopped at one family's wood shop, where we purchased several gifts as well as one rather sizeable nativity set to add to our own collection.

I'll tell you more about the places we visited in Bethlehem in the pages to come. Suffice it to say for the moment that this image of a not so little town of

Bethlehem complements my childlike imagination of a quaint, quiet little village. And maybe those of you who have visited there, or perhaps even lived or studied there, might have other images that come to your mind's eyes.

Isaac Villegas is a Mennonite pastor in North Carolina. He offers another contemporary image of Bethlehem. He describes visiting a refugee camp at Aida just outside Bethlehem in 2016. At one point he played soccer with some of the children on a field there near the wall that separates the cramped quarters of their occupied Palestinian side from the state of Israel on the other side. Israeli soldiers monitor Palestinian activity from watchtowers along the wall, and occasionally they will shoot tear gas canisters into the refugee camps to reinforce a sense of order and control. Some of the metal cylinders (which are marked "Made in the USA") hang in the mesh netting that covers the soccer field. Villegas realized that "to grow up in Aida Camp . . . is to live in a militarized valley of death, shadowed by soldiers on walls. Palestinian life can't escape the panoptic stare of the Israeli surveillance state, nor is there any respite from the threat of an army ready to disrupt the goings-on of a refugee city without warning. But the children still play soccer."[2]

---

[2] Villegas, "Tear gas," 33.

Bethlehem means different things to different people, and sometimes different things to the same person over time. Its meaning in the hearts and minds of people of faith has deepened over the years and across the scriptures. That evolution of Bethlehem's significance in the Bible leading up to Jesus's birth is what I am hoping to trace in these reflections.

A Thin Place

Nicholas Blincoe is a novelist, playwright, and screenwriter who is married to Leila Sansour, a filmmaker from Bethlehem. They split their time living there and in London. He has written what he calls a biography of Bethlehem in which he suggests that "it began life as a buffer between the desert and farmland."[3]

I'm drawn to this image of Bethlehem as a buffer land. Perhaps this resonates with the year my wife and I spent in Cornwall in the southwestern tip of England. Fresh out of seminary, I accepted a one-year appointment serving five British Methodist chapels in and around the town of Penzance (yes, it is a real place with a history of piracy, and it doesn't just exist in the imagination of Gilbert and Sullivan).

---

[3] Blincoe, *Bethlehem*, 5.

We lived about eight miles from Land's End, which is the closest point between the so-called old country and the new. The Cornish coastline was stunning. Rolling green farmland squared off by granite stone hedges jutted out over high brown cliffs along jagged lines above the surging waters of the north Atlantic, whose subtle shades of aquamarine changed with the seasons and the sun and the clouds. Artists and painters have long come to Cornwall to practice their craft and ply their trade, because there is just something unique about the quality of light in that place.

Cornwall, along with Ireland, Scotland, and Wales, is Celtic country. It was so far away from the mainland that the first-century Roman invaders pretty much left them alone. The ancient Celts were known for their concept of "thin places." These are essentially buffer zones. In-between places. Places where the lines—between land and sky and sea, between the material and the spiritual, between the visible and the invisible worlds—become blurred. They are places of physical as well as metaphysical convergence. They are natural places where we can encounter a sense of the supernatural, a sense of the sacred.

If, as Blincoe suggests, Bethlehem is a buffer zone that straddles the line between desert and farmland, then perhaps it is also one of the thin places of this world. Its geography seems appropriate for the birthplace of the one who straddled the line between humanity and divinity, the one who would lead us from the aridity of the desert of sin and death into the fertility of the fields of life and faith. Perhaps its existence as a thin place helps to explain the enduring lure of Bethlehem in our hearts and minds.

A Journey to Bethlehem

So let us make a journey in the imagination of our hearts and minds to Bethlehem this Advent season as we make our way to the celebration of our Savior's birth at Christmas. In the chapters to come, we will trace Bethlehem's presence and significance in the scriptures from Genesis to the Gospels.

We won't be able to cover all the appearances of Bethlehem in the biblical narrative. We won't, for example, review the undeniable bravery of King David's mighty warriors who snuck past the Philistine encampment to snag some water from the well in Bethlehem for their commander (2 Sam 23:13–17). Nor will we examine the undeniable brutality of the story of the Levite and his concubine from Bethlehem (Judg 19). Those are stories for another study. But the stories I have selected for us to study here point in some way toward the significance of the one whose birth we celebrate at Christmas.

These reflections were originally developed as an Advent sermon series in 2014 inspired by my visit to Bethlehem on our Holy Land pilgrimage earlier that year. As the war between Israel and Hamas broke out on my fiftieth birthday in 2023, I was inspired to revisit these reflections for another sermon series that following Advent season. As I have reflected on these Bethlehem stories most recently, I have come to discover that their themes generally correspond to the traditional themes for the four Sundays of Advent—hope, love, joy, and peace.

For those who might want to incorporate these reflections into your own private devotional practices or into the worship life of your congregations, I have included Advent wreath lighting liturgies before each chapter. These liturgies are based on the verses of Rev. Phillips Brooks' beloved carol "O Little Town of Bethlehem" that I first learned singing along with my mom at the piano. Each of the chapters also concludes with some questions geared toward both personal reflection and small group reflection, except for the last chapter, where I invite us to engage in the practice of breaking bread—whether at the Lord's table, in a Love Feast, or gathered with family and friends—in thanksgiving for the "house of bread" that is Bethlehem.

To deepen our experience of the scriptural and spiritual journey to the Bethlehem of Jesus' birth, I would invite you to consider also incorporating a physical dimension of this journey. It's estimated that Mary and Joseph would have traveled about ninety miles by foot from Nazareth in Galilee in the north to Bethlehem in Judah in the south (Luke 2:4). Depending on when the four Sundays of Advent fall on the calendar, the season of Advent can run from twenty-one days (starting on December 3) to twenty-eight days (starting on November 27). During the season of Advent, consider how you might incorporate a ninety-mile journey of some sort—by foot, by bike, by kayak, by skateboard or scooter, or by some combination of these or some other means—as a way of recalling Mary and Joseph's own Advent journey, and as a way of commemorating in our own flesh and bones the advent of the Son of God, the Word of God, in flesh and bone.

Finally, because God's gift of God's own self for us in the child born in Bethlehem inspires us to give of our own selves for others in his name, the proceeds from this study will go to support the Bethlehem Center in Chattanooga. Affectionately called "The Beth," the Bethlehem Center serves as a beacon of hope in the Chattanooga community by providing access to spiritual growth, education, leadership development, and other resources for at-risk children, youth, and families to overcome the vicious cycles of poverty and to experience the abundance of life in community that Christ offers. This ministry traces its beginnings back to 1920, and it grew out of Methodist lay and clergywomen like Rev. Sallie Crenshaw and Mrs. Miriam Brock coming together to make a difference in the lives of others in need. Your participation in this Advent study helps the Bethlehem Center continue to help others to thrive.

For more information on this ministry, visit https://www.thebeth.org.

First Sunday of Advent

Hope

O little town of Bethlehem, how still we see thee lie;
Above thy deep and dreamless sleep the silent stars go by.
Yet in thy dark streets shineth the everlasting light;
The hopes and fears of all the years are met in thee tonight.[4]

Rev. Phillips Brooks is regarded as one of America's greatest preachers.[5] When he was pastoring the Holy Trinity Episcopal Church in Philadelphia in 1865, he went on a pilgrimage to the Holy Land. He happened to be there during the Christmas season. On Christmas Eve, he traveled the six miles from Jerusalem to Bethlehem on horseback, passing through fields where he observed that shepherds were still keeping watch over their flocks by night. Then he attended the Christmas Eve worship service in the ancient Church of the Nativity, one of Christianity's oldest churches.

A couple of years after he returned from his trip, and as he continued to reflect upon his memorable night in Bethlehem, he felt inspired to compose a song for the children of his church to sing in their upcoming Christmas program. He then asked his organist, Lewis

---

[4] Brooks, *United Methodist Hymnal,* 230.
[5] Morgan, *Then Sings My Soul,* 167. See also Osbeck, *101 Hymn Stories,* 187–188.

Redner, to set the words he wrote to a tune the children could easily learn to sing. The tune came to him in a flash of inspiration the night before the performance, and Rev. Brooks named the tune "St. Louis" after his organist (but he changed the spelling so as not to embarrass the organist).

Bethlehem is no longer a little town—it is a busy city with a 2016 population of approximately 210,000 people.[6] And with all the unrest in the Palestinian West Bank where it is located, it doesn't lie very still these days. Yet "the hopes and fears of all the years" still meet there in the birthplace of Jesus the Messiah.

We light this first candle on our Advent wreath as a sign of our abiding hope that in the dark streets of this world, and even in our own hearts, the everlasting light of the holy child born in Bethlehem will shine still.

---

[6] Blincoe, *Bethlehem*, 193.

A Mother's Voice from Bethlehem

Genesis 35:16–20

Then they journeyed from Bethel, and when they were still some distance from Ephrath, Rachel was in childbirth, and she had hard labor. [17] When she was in her hard labor, the midwife said to her, "Do not be afraid, for now you have another son." [18] As her soul was departing, for she was dying, she named him Benoni, but his father called him Benjamin. [19] And Rachel died, and she was buried on the way to Ephrath, that is, Bethlehem, [20] and Jacob set up a pillar at her grave; it is the pillar of Rachel's tomb, which is there to this day.

The first mention of Bethlehem in the Bible is this somber story about the death and burial of one of the matriarchs in the family of Israel. But even this sad story hints of the salvation that would come to the world through the one born centuries later in the place where she was buried.

Rachel was the patriarch Jacob's favorite wife. They met at a well where she had brought the sheep she was keeping for her father Laban. It was love at first sight. Even though they were first cousins (Rachel was the daughter of Jacob's mother Rebekah's brother Laban), Jacob arranged with Laban to work for him for seven years in exchange for her hand in marriage. The time passed by quickly; the seven years "seemed to (Jacob) but a few days because of the love he had for her" (Gen 29:20).

When Jacob's seven years of service was up, Laban threw a feast and put on a wedding banquet for the whole town. But the night of the wedding, the father of the bride pulled a switcheroo and sent Rachel's older sister Leah into the honeymoon suite instead of Rachel. Jacob was, of course, none too pleased about this deception, and he told Laban so the next morning. Laban's response was that it's just "not done in our country" to marry off the younger before the older (Gen 29:26). So he proposed Jacob work another seven years for him and then he could have Rachel as his wife as well. Jacob was so enamored of Rachel that he readily agreed to this arrangement, and after that second seven-year period, he took her as his wife as well.

We're told that Jacob loved Rachel more than Leah, but Rachel had a hard time having children (Gen 29:30–31). Meanwhile, Leah was popping out babies left and right, hoping that her fertility would win Jacob's heart and warm him to her. The names Leah gave to her sons expressed her hope that he would draw closer to her. For example, she named her first born son Reuben, after the Hebrew word for "to see," for she said, "Because the Lord has looked on my affliction; surely now my husband will love me" (Gen 29:32).

Rachel became quite envious of her sister and also quite upset with Jacob. She blamed him for her infertility, and then he, in turn, blamed God (Gen 30:2). It's like Adam and Eve in the Garden all over again, passing the blame from one to the other. But then just like Jacob's grandmother Sarah let her husband Abraham go to their slave Hagar in hopes of producing children through her (Gen 16:1–6), Rachel allowed Jacob to sleep with her maid Bilhah in the hopes of producing children for him through her. History has a way of repeating itself in Genesis and in general.

This only fueled the sibling rivalry even more. Leah showed that two can play that game. She allowed Jacob to go to her maid Zilpah. Each of the maids bore two sons for Jacob. Leah went on to have two more sons for Jacob, for a total of six, plus a daughter Dinah. Finally, after all this time and tension in the family and torture in Rachel's heart, "God remembered Rachel, and God heeded her and opened her womb," and she conceived and bore a son whom she named Joseph (Gen 30:22–24).

The time came for Jacob's family to leave his wives' family home and return to his own family home. Jacob avenged his father-in-law's prior trickery by pulling a switcheroo of his own with some genetic engineering of Laban's livestock which left Jacob with the stronger mixed breeds and Laban with the weaker purebreds. Laban probably could have benefited from a basic course in biology.

As they were making their way down south to Jacob's homeland, probably following the path that became known as the Way of the Patriarchs that another couple expecting a child might have followed more than a millennium and a half later, we learn that Jacob's beloved wife Rachel once again became pregnant, expecting her second child. That's where the story picks up in this passage of scripture in which Bethlehem is mentioned for the first time in the Bible.

They were making their way south from Bethel, which is a special place in Jacob's story. That was where he had his dream of a ladder extending all the way up to heaven with angels traversing and where he received God's promise of the land (Gen 28:10–17). It was also where, after reconciling with his estranged brother Esau, he built an altar to the Lord, a pillar of stone, and named the place Bethel, which means the house of God (Gen 35:1–15, cf. 28:18–22).

They still had not reached Ephrath, which we learn a few verses later may have been an earlier, local, or family name for Bethlehem, when Rachel was in the midst of childbirth. Not only was she in labor, but the scripture specifies that she was having a hard labor (Gen 35:16). However, she was not alone. Her midwife was there, and she was trying to comfort Rachel and encourage her. "Don't be afraid," she told the struggling mother, "for you are having another son." But just as Rachel's soul was departing, or as some versions have it, as her life was fading away (CEB), or with her last breath (NLT), she named her son Benoni. But his father, that is, Jacob, called him Benjamin, and that's the name we know him by.

Then Rachel died, a fact that we're actually told two times in these two verses (v. 18–19). She was buried, we're told, on the way to Ephrath, which the passage clarifies for us is also Bethlehem. This is the first mention of Bethlehem in the Bible. It's identified as the location of Rachel's burial. Jacob sets up a pillar at her grave and we're told that the pillar "is there to this day" (Gen 35:20).

When my wife and I went to Bethlehem years ago, our group did not go to the site that is revered as Rachel's tomb, but we saw the road sign pointing in its direction. That the site is still honored nearly four thousand years later testifies to Rachel's prominence in Israel's memory.

Rachel's Reverberations

Rachel's poignant story clearly resonated with the people of Israel, because it is a story that is remembered a few more times in the Bible. First, later in the book of Genesis, when Jacob is sick and on his deathbed, he blesses Joseph's two sons Ephraim and Manasseh. He recalls for them how their grandmother "Rachel, alas, died in the land of Canaan . . . and I buried her there on the way to Ephrath," which the passage again clarifies as referring to Bethlehem (Gen 48:7). Just in that little word "alas," you can sense the depth of Jacob's grieving love over his beloved wife's death.

Fast-forward several centuries to the sixth century BCE when Jerusalem was defeated and destroyed by the Babylonians and the people of Judah were being deported, carried off into exile into Babylon. As they were making their slow, sad way out of Judah, the despondent people might have passed right by the beloved matriarch Rachel's tomb. The prophet Jeremiah imagines Rachel's voice crying out from the grave.

Thus says the Lord:
A voice is heard in Ramah,
lamentation and bitter weeping.
Rachel is weeping for her children;
she refuses to be comforted for her children,

because they are no more (Jer 31:15).[7]

For the prophet Jeremiah, Rachel's grief over her death in childbirth becomes a metaphor for the nation's grief over its defeat and the loss of its children, its future. Even though the prophet, like Rachel's midwife, goes on to offer an encouraging word from the Lord, that they shouldn't weep or mourn, for there is hope that their children shall return from the land of the enemy to their homeland, it's the image of Rachel refusing such quick and easy comfort that lingers in our minds (Jer 31:16–17).

Fast-forward another six hundred years or so, and the Gospel of Matthew remembers Rachel again when describing the paranoid King Herod's furious order to slaughter all the children living in and around Bethlehem who were two years old or younger after he had learned from the magi that a new king had been born in Bethlehem. That is a part of the Christmas story that we don't normally include in our children's Christmas pageants. "Who wants to play Herod this year?" asked no children's director ever. And aside from the haunting sixteenth century English "Coventry Carol," there aren't really any Christmas

---

[7] It is not clear to what Ramah refers. It could be the village between Bethel and Jerusalem, which places it at some distance from Bethlehem, or it could simply refer to a high place (as in "a voice was heard from on high").

carols referring to Herod's murderous rage. Neither Bing Crosby nor Mariah Carey ever sang about the slaughter of the innocent children. And yet when Matthew set about to describe the imperial response to the news of Jesus' birth, he remembered Rachel and her tears, and he referred to Jeremiah's ancient prophecy, which he saw fulfilled once more (Matt 2:17–18). So as we sing the bright words of "Hark! the Herald Angels Sing" and "Joy to the World," Matthew will not let us forget the loud lamentation of Rachel's weeping and wailing for her children all over again and refusing to be consoled.

Just as the place of Rachel's death was also the place of Benjamin's birth, so it is that the place of Jesus' birth became the place of the death of so many children. The popular author and pastor Adam Hamilton estimates that the size of Bethlehem in the first century might have meant that only a dozen or so children would have been affected by Herod's order, but even so, that's a dozen or so mothers whose weeping and wailing over their lost children would have been joined to Rachel's lamentations.[8]

One of the theologians I encountered when I was in seminary was Christopher Morse. He emphasizes the importance of what he calls faithful disbelief. Broadly

---

[8] Hamilton, *Journey*, 125.

speaking, he argues that not only is it important to believe the things about God and Jesus and the Bible and such that are true and right, it is also important to *disbelieve* the things that are false and wrong. He sees in Rachel's story a model of faithful refusal of easy explanations and false comfort in the face of the evil and suffering that we encounter, whether that be mothers dying in childbirth or parents whose children are deported or disappeared or die at the behest of oppressive powers and murderous tyrants. "In each of these three instances [of the scriptural references to her] the figure of Rachel personifies the human encounter with whatever in nature and history seeks to destroy the hope of the world."[9]

Sadly, these kinds of events in which Rachel's lamentations reverberate do not remain in the distant past. How readily we can imagine Rachel's voice crying out from the grave today, weeping and wailing over all the children carried off from their homes and families and communities, or held hostage, or abused or gravely injured or killed outright, in Bethlehem, in the West Bank, in Gaza, throughout Israel, in Ukraine, in Afghanistan, in Sudan, and in far too many places around the world. Rachel's voice resounds the world around, but her steadfast refusal to be comforted has seemed to insufficiently discomfort the world to do

---

[9] Morse, *Not Every Spirit*, 10.

much to resolve it. After all these years, have our ears become deaf to Rachel's loud lament?

A Change of Names

Let's go back to where it all began, to the original story in Genesis of Rachel's death in childbirth. What stands out in my mind in that story is the changing of the name of the child Rachel bore. She had given her son one name, but then Jacob came along and called him something else. What's that about?

Name changes are fairly common in the world of the Bible, as well as in our world. Abram became Abraham. Sarai became Sarah. Jacob became Israel. Simon became Peter. Saul became Paul. I remember when we were children my brother Dan wanted to change his name to Chevrolet (apparently he was demonstrating his *auto*-nomy). So changes of people's names happen all the time.

I went back and read back through the story of Jacob's family, and I saw that all of Jacob's children were named by their mothers. Even the children born by the surrogate mothers Bilhah and Zilpah were named by the women who were counted as their mothers, either Leah or Rachel. None of the children was named by their father Jacob—none of them, that is, except this last one.

As she lay there dying, as her soul was departing from her, with her last breath, Rachel named her son Ben-oni. It's a name that means Son of my Sorrow or Son of my Suffering. But Jacob called him Benjamin. That name means Son of the Right Hand, or Son of the South. Why did he do that? Why did he change the name his dying wife gave to her child on her death bed? Why didn't he respect her dying wish and leave the boy's name alone?

I wonder was it because he didn't want the child's name—Son of my Sorrow, Son of my Suffering—to be a constant reminder to him of her sorrow and suffering? Or to be a constant reminder of his own sorrow and suffering in losing her like that? Maybe he could not bear to handle his son's name being a constant reminder of his grief and loss. Was that why he changed the name to something more positive, that would refer to how close his relationship would be to this boy, that he would be like his right hand? Or even to something relatively neutral, referring to his being born during their southern sojourn, instead of something negative, something painful and sad?

I don't pretend to know what might have motivated Jacob to change the name his beloved wife Rachel gave to their last child. But I do know that we can do some strange things when we are grieving. And so I believe I can relate in some sense to what Jacob did. Maybe he did what a lot of us do when we try in many and various ways to put a positive spin on a negative experience. To put a happy, or at least happier, face upon a sad time. To gloss over some of the duller and darker moments in our lives with a little bit brighter paint if we can. We do it because sometimes we don't know exactly what to do with our sadness, our sorrow, our suffering, and our struggle, and especially with our grief. It's just so much easier to change its name. To call it something else, if we call it anything at all.

In this season of the year, we can feel a lot of pressure in our culture to put on a happy face, when it might in fact be a very sad time, a difficult time for us. It may not always feel like "the most wonderful time of the year." The world seems to want us to feel all merry and bright, when all we really feel is all messy and blue.

What would it mean for us to do our best to honor Rachel's memory and to name whatever heaviness, messiness, sorrow, or sadness we may be facing or feeling this season, and not to let anyone else or even ourselves try to change its name, but to call it what it is, by name, and to let that be its name?

What sorrow or sadness or loss have you experienced that you would want to name this Advent season? Maybe you have had difficulty having children, or maybe you have lost a pregnancy, or a child. Maybe you have lost a parent, or a spouse, or a marriage. Maybe you have lost your job or your home. Maybe you have lost your health. Maybe you have lost your hopes and dreams for a different or better life. Maybe you have lost a sense of meaning and purpose and direction in your life. Maybe you have lost a sense of safety, security, and stability. Maybe you have lost your faith and trust in someone else.

And maybe, like Rachel, you refuse to be comforted by some of the pious platitudes that too often pass for Christian caregiving, like "everything happens for a reason" or "the Lord must have needed another angel in heaven" or "whenever God closes one door, he opens another." Folks may mean well when they say such things to us, and we may mean well when we say things like that to others. But when we do that, we're in danger of doing the very same thing Jacob did: changing its name, calling it something brighter, sunnier, to make if not others then at least ourselves feel better.

A Modern Day Rachel

Several years ago, I met a clergy colleague for lunch at a Cracker Barrel restaurant. The waitress came to take our order. My friend saw her name tag and said to her, "Renee, here in a few minutes we are going to say a prayer over our meal, and I just wondered if there was anything you might like us to pray for." Well, Renee set her coffee pot right down on our table and said, "You don't know how much I need prayer right now. My mom is in the ICU and I'm a single mom with two kids just trying to do the best I can." I could hear the fatigue in her voice and saw the tears welling up in her eyes as she went on to say, "You know, they say that God doesn't give us more than we can handle. But you know, I'm not so sure about that." Then she picked her coffee pot back up. But before she left the table, my friend thanked her for sharing that with us, and he assured her we would pray for her and her mom and her family.

I was thinking about Renee and what she said as I was making my way back home. I wasn't so sure I believed that old saying about God not giving us more than we can handle either. In fact, I don't think it's true. I don't think God acts that way at all. I don't believe that the bad things that happen in our lives are always God's fault, or that God gives them to us or lets those things happen. Sometimes awful things just happen. Sometimes it's our fault; sometimes it's somebody else's fault; sometimes it's nobody's fault. And I have come to learn that sometimes we can have more things going on in our lives than anyone can reasonably be expected to handle.

I'm grateful to Renee for saying what she said, for questioning the old cliché. It reminded me of Rachel, a kindred spirit who likewise refused to be consoled by the easy explanations and the false comforts, who called it like it was, who died with the name she had given her son on her lips, Ben-oni, Son of my Sorrow.

Two Names Become One

What sorrow or sadness or loss would you name this year? What if you wrote its name—whatever its name is, whatever name you would want to give it—down on a piece of paper and placed it in the manger of the one whose birth in Bethlehem we celebrate this season?

Because the good news, for you, for me, for Renee, and even for Rachel, though she couldn't have known it at the time, is that the baby born in Bethlehem centuries after Rachel was buried there is Emmanuel, God with us. That is the deep and abiding hope of this season. In Jesus Emmanuel, God is with us. We are not alone. God is with us in our sorrow as well as in our joy. God is with us in our darkness as well as in our light. God is with us in our bluer Christmases as well as in our brighter ones. In Jesus Emmanuel, God is with us at the manger, God is with us at the cross, and God is with us at the empty tomb.

For it is through the death and resurrection of Jesus that the two names—the name Rachel gave her son and the name Jacob gave him—became one. It is precisely because Jesus is the Son of Suffering and Sorrow for us on the cross that he is ultimately revealed as the Son of the Right Hand of God through his resurrection from the dead. The Son of Suffering and Sorrow is the Son of the Right Hand. In Jesus, they are one and the same.

Questions for Reflection and Discussion

1. What does your name mean? How did you get your name? Have you ever wanted to change your name? What would you change it to?

2. Many women, like Rachel, want to have children but experience great difficulty in having children. What can the church do to support and care for these women and families, especially at Christmas time, but also throughout the year?

3. How can we be more attentive and responsive to those in our congregations and in our broader culture for whom this season is a difficult time? What are some ways we can honor their struggle and offer hope?[10]

---

[10] The reflections in this chapter were originally crafted for a "Blue Christmas" worship service. Such worship services are often held on the longest night of the year, December 21 or 22, and so they are also known as "Longest Night" services. Resources for these services may be found online at

Second Sunday of Advent

Love

For Christ is born of Mary, and gathered all above,
While mortals sleep, the angels keep their watch of wondering love.
O morning stars together, proclaim the holy birth,
And praises sing to God the King, and peace to all on earth![11]

Advent is a season of watching and waiting. Not only are we preparing to celebrate the first coming of Christ in his birth in Bethlehem long ago, but we are also still awaiting his second coming, his return in glory to establish his everlasting reign here on earth as it is in heaven.

But no one knows when that time will be. Even Jesus himself said "neither the angels in heaven, nor the Son, but only the Father" knows when that day will be (Mark 13:32). So Jesus tells us to keep watch, to stay awake, and to be always alert for signs of his coming, his arrival among us.

---

https://www.umcdiscipleship.org/resources/blue-christmaslongest-night-worship-with-those-who-mourn or https://www.ministrymatters.com/all/entry/3053/longest-night.

[11] Brooks, *United Methodist Hymnal*, 230.

In the second verse of this beloved Christmas carol "O Little Town of Bethlehem," the angels are the ones who keep watch while the rest of us mortals sleep. Even though the image of angels watching over us might help us to sleep more peacefully at night, Advent is an invitation for us mortals to awaken from all the busy-ness and the stress of the season that can keep us spiritually asleep, and to join the angels in keeping "their watch of wondering love."

We light this second Advent candle, and we pray that God would open the eyes of our hearts this season, that we may be watchful, in a spirit of wonder, for the redeeming love that journeyed to us long ago and sojourns among us still.

A Redeemer in Bethlehem

Ruth 4:7–12

⁷Now this was the custom in former times in Israel concerning redeeming and exchanging to confirm a transaction: the one took off a sandal and gave it to the other; this was the manner of attesting in Israel. ⁸So when the next-of-kin said to Boaz, "Acquire it for yourself," he took off his sandal. ⁹Then Boaz said to the elders and all the people, "You are witnesses today that I have acquired from the hand of Naomi all that belonged to Elimelech and all that belonged to Chilion and Mahlon. ¹⁰I have also acquired Ruth the Moabite, the wife of Mahlon, to be my wife, to maintain the dead man's name on his inheritance, in order that the name of the dead may not be cut off from his kindred and from the gate of his native place; today you are witnesses." ¹¹Then all the people who were at the gate, along with the elders, said, "We are witnesses. May the Lord make the woman who is coming into your house like Rachel and Leah, who together built up the house of Israel. May you produce children in Ephrathah and bestow a name in Bethlehem;¹² and, through the children that the Lord will give you by this young woman, may your house be like the house of Perez, whom Tamar bore to Judah."

When Tracy and I went on our pilgrimage to the Holy Land, there were a few other pastors in our tour group. Together, we took turns offering daily devotions for the group at the various sites we visited. My turn fell on the day we were scheduled to visit Bethlehem.

After visiting the Church of the Nativity—the ancient church built over the traditional location of Jesus' birth—we went to the nearby Shepherds' Fields where contemporary shepherds still keep watch over their sheep by day and by night. In fact, as we were pulling into the parking area in our tour bus, I recall seeing one of them talking on a cell phone—a twenty-first century device that the first-century shepherds certainly lacked (and perhaps they were better off for not having it!). Carved into the hillsides are caves, some of which have been enclosed in glass where tour groups can gather. It was inside one of those caves that I was to deliver my devotion.

Our tour guide was a Palestinian Christian who had been leading tours there for over twenty years. He caught me early on the day of my devotion and asked me if I were going to talk about Ruth and Boaz. I must have looked at him like he had asked if I had three heads. I said no, I was planning on talking about the shepherds keeping watch over their flocks the night of Jesus' birth. I mean, here we were in the Shepherds' Fields and all. Hello! The only thing I knew about Ruth and Boaz was what kind of a man Boaz was before he got married: Ruthless. He seemed disappointed. Not in my bad dad joke, but that I wasn't talking about Ruth and Boaz.

Actually, I did know a little about Ruth and Boaz. One spring when I was in the fifth grade, my home church's children's ministry put on a play about the story of Ruth. I was assigned the part of Boaz, and playing my beautiful wife Ruth was this fourth grader with long blonde hair named Heidi. Her dad was our church's choir director. Maybe I was experiencing an unaware attempt at method acting, but I thought she was the cutest girl in the whole church, and I certainly didn't mind at all that she was my stage wife. That summer, she and her family moved away. Her dad got a new job at a church in Cookeville, Tennessee. I had no idea where that was, but I was pretty sure it was the other end of the earth.

But back to the Holy Land. Our tour guide's question piqued my interest. I did some more digging into that story. I already knew that you can't really talk about the story of Jesus without talking about the place he was born, Bethlehem. But I have come to appreciate that you can't really talk about the significance of Bethlehem in the Bible without talking about the story of Ruth.

The Story of Ruth

Ruth is one of only two books in the Bible named for a woman (the other is Esther). But even though the book is named for Ruth, the story is really about her mother-in-law Naomi.

The story takes place back in the days before there were kings, back when the various judges ruled over the people of Israel. There was a family of four—a man named Elimelech (which means "God is my king" in Hebrew), his wife Naomi, and their two sons Mahlon and Chilion—and they lived in Bethlehem (not the town in Pennsylvania).

There came a famine in the land, so this family of four decided to leave Bethlehem (again, which means "House of Bread" in Hebrew) for neighboring Moab to go find bread. Now this is somewhat ironic for them to leave Bethlehem, the house of bread, to look for bread. That's a little bit like leaving Tennessee to look for volunteers.

It wasn't just that Moab was another country. The people of Judah looked down on the Moabites, because they were descendants, along with the Ammonites, of an incestuous relationship involving the patriarch Abraham's nephew Lot and Lot's two daughters (Gen 19:30–38). So it was humiliating enough to have to leave Bethlehem, the house of bread, to look for bread, but it was even moreso to have to go to Moab (not the city in Utah).

While they were in Moab, Elimelech, the dad, died. The two sons married, but they married Moabite women. One was named Orpah, which happens to be the namesake of a very famous woman today who was originally named Orpah but her family kept mispronouncing and misspelling it, and so we know her as Oprah.[12]

The other Moabite woman was named Ruth.

After they'd lived in Moab for about ten years, both of Naomi's sons died. Their names prophesied their sad fate: Mahlon means "sickness" and Chilion means "wasting away." So Naomi was without a husband or sons, and in a patriarchal culture, that was a particularly vulnerable situation both for her and for her daughters-in-law.

Naomi got word that there was bread again back in Bethlehem, the house of bread, so she resolved to return home to the land of Judah. Both of her daughters-in-law set out to go there with her, but Naomi encouraged them to return to their own homes and try to find new husbands and new lives for

---

[12] https://www.americannamesociety.org/about-names-why-oprah-winfrey-has-such-a-rare-first-name/

themselves. She also might have wanted to spare them the probable prejudice they might have encountered as Moabite women coming to Judah. Initially, they protested that they were sticking with her. But Naomi insisted that there's nothing she could do for them, no new sons that she could give as husbands to them. Orpah eventually relented and reluctantly returned to her home. Naomi tried to get Ruth to follow suit, but in what is probably the best-known passage in the book, Ruth pledged her loyalty to her mother-in-law:

Do not press me to leave you
or to turn back from following you!
Where you go, I will go;
where you lodge, I will lodge;
your people shall be my people,
and your God my God.
Where you die, I will die—
there will I be buried.
May the Lord do thus and so to me,
and more as well,
if even death parts me from you! (1:16–17)

Naomi saw that she couldn't change Ruth's mind, so on they went.

When they arrived in Bethlehem, the people inquired, "Is this Naomi?" (1:19). But she told them not to call her Naomi (which means "pleasant") anymore, but instead to call her Mara (which means "bitter") because the Lord had dealt bitterly with her (1:20). She had gone away full, but now she had returned empty. She had left Bethlehem a pleasant person but returned bitter.

Maybe you are arriving in Bethlehem this Advent and Christmas season feeling a little like Naomi—bitter, hopeless, feeling empty, feeling like the Lord has dealt you a hard hand and called calamity upon you.

There Is A Redeemer

Ruth and Naomi happened to arrive back in Bethlehem at the beginning of the barley harvest. Ruth offered to go out into the fields and glean from among the grain. Gleaning was an ancient form of charity in which the poor, the widow, the orphan, and the alien (or foreigner) could come along after the harvesters and gather the leftovers (Lev 19:9, 23:22, Deut 24:19). It just so happened (which makes it sound like coincidence but perhaps we are meant to read providence instead) that she went to glean in the field belonging to a man named Boaz. And Boaz, as it happened, was a relative of Elimelech, Ruth's deceased father-in-law.

In one of the most memorable meet-cutes in the Bible, Ruth caught the eye of Boaz (which is not the town in Alabama), and he inquired among his field hands about her. They told him that she's the Moabite who returned with Naomi. Boaz went over to her and told her to stay in his fields, not to glean in any other fields. He also instructed his men not to bother her but to look after her and to give her whatever she needed. He even invited her to dine at the table with him at suppertime. She asked him why he was being so kind to her, since she was a foreigner, and he told her that he was impressed by her loyalty to her mother-in-law Naomi.

When she returned to Naomi with all the grain she had gathered, Naomi asked her in whose fields she gleaned. Ruth told her the man's name was Boaz. Naomi perked up at the mention of his name, and she praised the Lord for this bit of kindness towards them, for Boaz was a relative, a kinsman.

The word here for relative in Hebrew is *go'el*, which means one who has the right to redeem. Some form of the word *go'el* for redeemer or redeem appears over twenty times in the eighty-five verses of this book. To redeem literally means to buy back, to retrieve, or to recover what has been lost. In the patriarchal society of the time, in which inheritances are passed through the males in a family, the *go'el*—the near kinsman, as it's often translated in our English versions of the Bible—could marry into the family and redeem and restore for Naomi and Ruth all the property, protection, and provision that they had lost when their husbands had died.

So Naomi orchestrated a little romance. She told Ruth to clean up, freshen up, get all gussied up, splash a little perfume on her, and go find Boaz at the end of the harvest, after he'd finished celebrating and was relaxing. One of my clergy colleagues, Gary Ihfe, shared that this reminds him of that old song "Fancy" by Reba McEntire—"here's your one chance, Fancy, don't let me down!"

Ruth went and found Boaz there at the threshing floor, having eaten his fill and, like many of us after our Thanksgiving meals, "in a contented mood" (3:7). She went over to him and laid down next to him and essentially proposed marriage to him—quite an unlikely and unexpected thing for her to have done. She said to him, "I am Ruth, your servant; spread your cloak over your servant, for you are next-of-kin" (3:9). She asked him to enfold her into his care, for he was the *go'el*, the one who could redeem everything for them.

Boaz, as we could have already surmised, would have been all too happy to oblige, but he was also aware that there was another man who was closer kin to them than he was. Boaz told Ruth that they would have to check with that man first to see if he would be willing to act as her redeemer. That man would have the right of first refusal; after all, he was the first *go'el* (this reminds me of another Christmas carol!)

First thing in the morning, they made their way to the village gate where they happened upon the nearer kinsman. Boaz invited him over to sit with him, along with several of the city elders (to act as witnesses). Boaz informed the man that Naomi, the widow of their kinsman Elimelech, was about to sell some land, and that this fellow had the first option to buy the property. The man told Boaz he'd like to buy it. Then Boaz told him that there was a certain string attached, that along with the land would come Elimelech's daughter-in-law Ruth the Moabite. That was when the nearest kin changed his tune, saying he couldn't redeem their inheritance for them without jeopardizing his own inheritance. That may well have been true, but I also can't help but wonder if part of it had to do with the fact that Ruth was a Moabite.

The way then is cleared for Boaz to redeem the family name and property for Naomi and for Ruth. The two men confirmed the transaction with the nearer kinsman taking off his sandal and giving it to Boaz. Apparently, that was how such transactions were confirmed in ancient times; otherwise, the arrangement would be "sandal-less!"

A House Blessing

Then the people of the town of Bethlehem witnessed and blessed the joining together of Ruth and Boaz, and they prayed a blessing upon their house:

May the Lord make the woman who is coming into your house like Rachel and Leah, who together built up the house of Israel. May you produce children in Ephrathah and bestow a name in Bethlehem; and, through the children that the Lord will give you by this young woman, may your house be like the house of Perez, whom Tamar bore to Judah (4:11–12).

In other words, they prayed this blessing over their house—not just the physical structure, but the family, their descendants, that they may essentially become a dynasty.

Sure enough, in time, Ruth bore a son whose name was Obed. And in time, Obed had a son whose name was Jesse. And in time, Jesse had a son, whose name was David. And David became the greatest, most beloved king Israel has ever known. And it's to the story of David that we will turn next. Long before there ever was a Babe Ruth or a Yankee stadium, this is the house, the family, the dynasty that Ruth built.

And if you track David's genealogy on down the line, as the Gospel of Matthew does in its very first chapter, you eventually come to another baby boy born to a man and woman in Bethlehem—Jesus, who, not only as the so-called Son of David, but as the very Son of God, is the only one who truly has the right to redeem us, not only from shame and sorrow, from misery and misfortune, from bitterness and emptiness and hopelessness, but from the power of sin and death itself, to give us new life.

I don't know about you, but I love redemption stories—in books and movies, in tv shows, and in real life. The greatest redemption story of all is the story of God's redemption of the world through Jesus Christ. And this grand redemption story takes an important step forward in the redemption that took place a long time ago, in a land far, far away, in the little town of Bethlehem.

Questions for Reflection and Discussion

1. Do you have a favorite redemption story in a book, tv show or movie? Who is the redeemer? Who is redeemed? From what kind of situation are they redeemed?

2. How have you experienced redemption in your life? When have you needed to be restored, and who acted as your redeemer? When have you been positioned to act as a redeemer for someone else?

3. How would you describe the redemption that Christ offers to us? From what are we needing to be redeemed? How are we to respond to this redemption?

4. The redemptive power of kindness is a key theme in the story of Ruth, particularly the kindness shown to and by outsiders like Ruth the Moabite. When have you been shown kindness, particularly by someone you would consider an outsider who is different from you in some way? What can the church do to be more kind to those who might be considered, or who might consider themselves, outsiders? What kinds of kindness can you show to others, particularly outsiders?

Third Sunday of Advent

Joy

How silently, how silently, the wondrous gift is given;
So God imparts to human hearts the blessings of his heaven.
No ear may hear his coming, but in this world of sin,
Where meek souls will receive him, still the dear Christ enters
in.[13]

In this season of the year so filled with the sounds of songs being sung, bells being rung, and festivities being flung, it's curious that the writer of this beloved carol, Rev. Phillips Brooks, imagined the entry of the immortal God into human flesh on the face of the earth as taking place in sheer silence. "How silently," he wrote, and then repeated for emphasis, "how silently, the wondrous gift is given."

How utterly improbable that the Messiah slipped into the world incognito. He wasn't born in a royal palace but in an animal stall. Not in the bustling capital city, but in a small, quiet village. The first to receive the news of his birth wasn't the local media or the tabloid paparazzi, but day laborers working the night shift.

---

[13] Brooks, *United Methodist Hymnal*, 230.

Aside from Mary and Joseph, no one really knew. No ear could hear his coming.

The carol claims that's also how Christ enters the hearts of those who will receive him, not so much in big and boisterous ways, but more subtly, in silence, stillness. That is often when we are most receptive to the wondrous gift given to us in Christ.

Today we light this third candle on our Advent wreath, the pink candle which represents joy, as we continue to look and listen for the joy that comes to us, not in the noise, but beneath and beyond the noise, in the calm and the quiet, the stillness and the silence.

A New King in Bethlehem

1 Samuel 16:1–13

The Lord said to Samuel, "How long will you grieve over Saul? I have rejected him from being king over Israel. Fill your horn with oil and set out; I will send you to Jesse the Bethlehemite, for I have provided for myself a king among his sons." ² Samuel said, "How can I go? If Saul hears of it, he will kill me." And the Lord said, "Take a heifer with you and say, 'I have come to sacrifice to the Lord.' ³ Invite Jesse to the sacrifice, and I will show you what you shall do, and you shall anoint for me the one whom I name to you." ⁴ Samuel did what the Lord commanded and came to Bethlehem. The elders of the city came to meet him trembling and said, "Do you come peaceably?" ⁵ He said, "Peaceably. I have come to sacrifice to the Lord; sanctify yourselves and come with me to the sacrifice." And he sanctified Jesse and his sons and invited them to the sacrifice.

⁶ When they came, he looked on Eliab and thought, "Surely his anointed is now before the Lord." ⁷ But the Lord said to Samuel, "Do not look on his appearance or on the height of his stature, because I have rejected him, for the Lord does not see as mortals see; they look on the outward appearance, but the Lord looks on the heart." ⁸ Then Jesse called Abinadab and made him pass before Samuel. He said, "Neither has the Lord chosen this one." ⁹ Then Jesse made Shammah pass by. And he said, "Neither has the Lord chosen this one." ¹⁰ Jesse made seven of his sons pass before Samuel, and Samuel said to Jesse, "The Lord has not chosen any of these." [11] Samuel said to Jesse, "Are all your sons here?" And he said, "There remains yet the youngest, but he is keeping the sheep." And Samuel said to Jesse, "Send and bring him, for we will not sit down until he comes here." [12] He sent and brought him in. Now he was ruddy and had beautiful eyes and was handsome. The Lord said, "Rise and anoint him, for this is the one." [13] Then Samuel took the horn of oil and anointed him in the presence of his brothers, and the spirit of the Lord came mightily upon David from that day forward. Samuel then set out and went to Ramah.

When I was in eighth grade, I played on our junior high school basketball team. I had grown something like six inches in six months that year, and someone thought I should try out for the team. So I did, and I made it. I was the third-string center. I think I scored a total of eight points the whole season!

When the season was over and we had won the district championship, having beaten teams from bigger cities like Bristol, our coach took us out to dinner and a movie at the Bristol Mall. This was the nearest mall to our little town of Marion, about an hour's drive. I can't remember where we had dinner, but I won't forget the movie we watched together: *Hoosiers.*

It's a movie about a small-town high school basketball team in rural Indiana with a handful of guys on the team. Gene Hackman plays the new coach with the challenge not only of winning basketball games but winning over the hearts of the townspeople. After some unconventional coaching techniques and controversial gametime decisions, they do start winning games, and they win their way all the way to the state championship in Indianapolis.

In one of my favorite scenes, the team enters the ginormous gymnasium, looking up to the rafters with their mouths agape. The coach asks a couple of the players to get a tape measure and measure the height of the goal and the distance from the foul line. Same as their cozy gym back home in Hickory.

I don't mean to spoil the movie if you haven't seen it, but you can probably guess what happens. Small town team with smaller players goes up against big city team with much bigger players and wins the state championship with a last second shot! It's a classic underdog story, and those of us in the theatre that night saw ourselves in that story. That was, in a sense, our own story played out on the big screen before us.

The Bible contains some great underdog stories. There are the stories of Joseph, Moses, Ruth the Moabite, and Israel itself. There's the story of Jesus, of course, and his ragtag band of followers that became known as the church. But probably the most famous and best-known underdog story in the Bible is David and Goliath. The young shepherd boy, armed with only a sling and a few smooth stones, goes up against a Sherman tank of a soldier with full body armor and a sword the size of a redwood tree. And we all know how that story ends. But before there was *that* story, there was *this* story—the story of how David was chosen to become the next king of Israel. And it's an underdog story as well.

The Underdog Becomes the Top Dog

The story takes place when a man named Saul was the king. He was the very first king of Israel. He was anointed by a man named Samuel, who wore a lot of hats. He was a prophet, someone who communicates both with God on behalf of the people and with the people on behalf of God. A prophet was also called a "seer" at the time. We know he was a seer because he wears a seer-sucker suit! He was also a judge, which was a local leader among the people. And he was a kingmaker, one sent by God to anoint kings.

This last role was one Samuel served reluctantly. He didn't want to be a kingmaker. He tried to talk the people out of wanting a king. He told them that a king would only tax them, take their sons off to war and their daughters off to work, and take their fields and farm animals. But they wouldn't listen. They said they didn't care. They wanted to be like the other nations. They wanted a king! So God said to Samuel, "let them have a king. It's not you they're rejecting, it's me as their king. If they want a king so bad, I'll give them a king." Then God led Samuel to Saul to anoint him as the first king (1 Sam 8–10).

Saul was doing a pretty decent job as king until he started disobeying God and doing his own thing. For example, he presumed to take for himself the role of the priest and to offer a burnt offering to the Lord (1 Sam 13), and he spared the life of an enemy king against the Lord's explicit command of total destruction (1 Sam 15). Then the Lord became sorry for making Saul king and sent Samuel to go and anoint a new king for Israel. The Lord sent him to a man named Jesse in the little town of Bethlehem to anoint one of his sons as the next king.

Samuel made his way to Bethlehem, under the pretense that he was going there to offer a sacrifice in case word got back to Saul (who would have been none too happy to have heard of Samuel's errand). When he arrived in Bethlehem, the elders came out to meet him and inquired tremulously if he had come in peace. This was a reasonable question for them to ask, because the last anyone saw of Samuel was when he had to do what Saul wouldn't and sawed the enemy Amalekite King Agag into pieces (1 Sam 15:33). Samuel assured the

Bethlehemites that he had come peaceably to offer a sacrifice, and he instructed them to sanctify themselves.

When they had come together for the sacrifice, Samuel the seer looked on Jesse's oldest son Eliab and thought surely this was the one the Lord wanted him to anoint. After all, he was the oldest. And he had a good name—Eliab means "God is my father." But the Lord instructed Samuel the seer on how the Lord sees things. "Do not look on his appearance," the Lord told him, "or on how tall he is, because he's not the one. The Lord doesn't see things the way mortals do. They only see the outward appearance, but the Lord looks on the heart" (1 Sam 16:7). A person's heart, which was in ancient times the seat of the will, is more important than the person's height.

Then Jesse sent out the second oldest son, Abinadab. But it wasn't him. Then the third oldest Shammah. Not him either. After Jesse paraded seven of his sons before Samuel, none of whom was the chosen one, Samuel asked, probably with some confusion and consternation, "are these all your sons?" Jesse replied that there was actually one more, the youngest, but he was out keeping the sheep. Samuel told him to go fetch him, for they weren't sitting down to eat the sacrifice until he arrived.

When the youngest son arrived in from the fields, he's described with three physical features. First, he was ruddy, which means he has a healthy reddish glow. It could also mean he has red hair. Or maybe a red neck (would that have made him a redneck?). Second, he had beautiful eyes. Third, he was handsome. God said he's the one, anoint him.

But wait, didn't God just say that the Lord doesn't look on outward appearances? Yet here is all this talk about the young man's outward appearance, how he was a ruddy looker with dreamy eyes? The first king, Saul, was also described as a handsome fellow—there was no one more handsome in all Israel—who stood head and shoulders above everyone else (1 Sam 9:2). So while it may be the case that you can have both good looks and a good heart, what matters most to God is a good heart. When Samuel told Saul that he had fallen out of favor with God, he told him that the Lord was looking for a man after God's own heart (1 Sam 13:14). Apparently, the Lord found him in the youngest son of Jesse.

So Samuel took the horn of oil he'd brought with him and anointed David in the presence of his father and his brothers. The Hebrew word for anoint is used four times in these thirteen verses. It's the word *maschach*, from which we get the word messiah. The Greek word for anoint is *chrio*, from which we get Christ, from *christos*, the anointed one. Long before the Christ, the Messiah, the king of all creation, was born in Bethlehem, this young man, the youngest son, the little brother, was anointed as the next king of Israel.

What an occasion of joy and delight for Jesse and for David! But also what misery it must have been for his older brothers. Can you imagine how they must have felt after having been passed over for this honor by the runt of the litter? In "Eliab's complaint," the poet Philip Kolin imagines how the eldest brother Eliab might have reacted against this unconventional anointing.[14] "I had all the qualifications," he smarts. "How could my kid brother be anointed, / the one with rosacea" he asks incredulously. "My name alone should have given me / the edge in the kingdom." But again, God doesn't see things the way we see them. Even though Eliab's got a good name that means "God is my father," David's got a good name, too. It means "beloved."

It's strange, but we don't actually learn his name until the last verse in this passage. It's not that we haven't known his name all along, but the scripture doesn't drop his name until after he's anointed. "And the spirit of the Lord came mightily upon David from that day forward" (1 Sam 16:13). The Lord's spirit transferred

---

[14] Kolin, "Eliab's complaint."

from Saul to David, and from this point on in the narrative, Saul's star falls while the star of David rises, until he became the greatest king Israel has ever known. The underdog becomes the top dog.

In a way, this is a rather surprising story, but in another way, it's not a surprise at all. Up to this point, God has repeatedly demonstrated a peculiar fondness for the younger over the older—Abel over Cain, Isaac over Ishmael, Jacob over Esau—as well as for shepherds—Jacob, Moses, and now David. The rabbis used to say that "when God wishes to choose a leader, God looks to see how he tends sheep."[15] And sure enough, the descendant of David whose birth in Bethlehem we celebrate this season called himself "the good shepherd (who) lays down his life for the sheep" (John 10:11). And like the babies of the family, shepherds are seen as lower class, lesser than, underdogs. Why this tendency of God to choose the unexpected, the unlikely, the underdogs?

Perhaps it has something to do with what God said to Samuel the seer about how the Lord see things. The Lord doesn't see things the way we see things. We look at the outward appearance. We see only the surface. But the Lord looks deeper. The Lord looks underneath the surface. The Lord looks on the heart.

---

[15] Wolpe, *David*, 2.

A Matter of the Heart

So much of our lives are lived out at the surface level of appearances, especially this time of the year. We work hard to make the decoration of our homes bright and perfect. We create and send Christmas cards with shining and smiling faces, showing happy families. We curate our social media posts to show others what we want them to see and thus to think about us. We spend so much time and energy and money on "keeping up appearances" (to borrow from the name of an old British sitcom) when what really matters to God is what's on the inside, what's in our hearts.

This leads me to a question: if it is true that the Lord doesn't see things the way we do, that the Lord doesn't look at outward appearances but instead looks on our hearts, then what did God see when God looked at David's heart?

Even though David would grow up and become Israel's greatest king, the scripture doesn't hide that he had some heart problems. He had a lustful heart that led to adultery, murder, and a broken marriage. He had a broken heart when his own sons turned against him and tried to take the throne from him. Like his royal predecessor, David would come to know failure as a king, as a husband, as a father, and as a warrior. He had a troubled heart, a conflicted heart. Yet through it all, he maintained a heart after God's own heart. In one of the many psalms attributed to his hand, he prayed, "Create in me a clean heart, O God, and put a new and right spirit within me" (Ps 51:10). David trusted in a God who looks at the heart and does not despise "a broken and contrite heart" (Ps 51:17).

Many years later, when the time came for a new king to be found in Bethlehem, God came again to a pair who, by all outward appearances, would have been unlikely, unexpected, underdogs. He was a common carpenter; she was a nobody from a nothing town that wasn't even on the maps. But the Lord looked on his heart and saw a kindness and compassion that refused to hurt even one whom he thought might have done him harm (Matt 1:19). And the Lord looked on her heart and saw how deeply she treasured and pondered things in her heart (Luke 2:19, 51).

And the child they would raise together became a young man who had a penchant for looking beyond all outward appearances and peering into the heart. He would choose the unlikely and unexpected to be his disciples, not the religious leaders or scholars, but common folks, fishermen, even a despised tax collector. And he would say that it's not what goes in our mouths that defile us but what comes out, because what comes out of our mouths comes from the heart

(Matt 15:10–20, Mark 7:14–23). It's what's in the heart that matters, that is most important.

Jesus had a way of seeing into people's hearts. In one scene that three of the four Gospels recount, a fellow, who apparently was fairly wealthy and may have been young and may have been a ruler, comes up to Jesus and asks him what he needs to do to inherit eternal life (Matthew 19:16–30, Mark 10:17–31, Luke 18:18–30). Jesus tells him to keep the commandments, and then lists a few of the Big Ten (not the college athletic conference but the Ten Commandments). The man tells Jesus he's kept them all since his youth. Then, in Mark's version, we're told that Jesus looks at him and loves him (Mark 10:21). I like to think that when Jesus looked at the man with love, he was looking into his heart, because he saw what was holding the man back, and he says so. "You lack one thing," he told the man. "Go, sell what you own, and give the money to the poor, and you will have treasure in heaven; then come, follow me." But the guy couldn't do it. He couldn't let go of all he had. So he went away grieving. I suspect his heart was heavy because he knew Jesus saw right into it.

The season of Advent is a season of preparation, of preparing not just our homes and our hearths, but most importantly, our hearts. It's a time to make room for the new king in Bethlehem to be born even more fully in our hearts. When the Lord, who sees things differently than we see them, who looks not on our outward appearance but on our hearts, looks at your heart, what do you think the Lord sees? And how might we open our hearts to being changed, being transformed, being anointed anew and afresh with the spirit of joy over the new king born in Bethlehem, Jesus the Christ?

Questions for Reflection and Discussion

1. What is your favorite underdog story, and why is it so meaningful to you?

2. Do you have brothers or sisters? Where are you in the lineup? Have you ever experienced a time when you were jealous of a sibling, or maybe of a classmate or colleague or close friend, over some honor or accolade you thought you deserved instead of them? How can our jealousy of others be overcome by joy for others?

3. What do you think God saw in David's heart that would make him such a good leader for God's people? What do you think God sees in your heart that God can use for the glory of God and the good of others?

4. Jesus said, "Blessed are the pure in heart, for they shall see God" (Matt 5:8). What do you think he means by that?

Fourth Sunday of Advent

Peace

O holy Child of Bethlehem, descend to us, we pray;
Cast out our sin, and enter in, be born in us today.
We hear the Christmas angels the great glad tidings tell;
O come to us, abide with us, our Lord Emmanuel![16]

The final verse of this beloved Christmas carol shifts from language *about* Jesus to language directed *toward* Jesus. It's a shift from telling the story of Jesus and his birth to saying a prayer to Jesus at his birth.

One of the things that this verse and good prayers have in common is a lot of verbs! Verbs are action words. They are all about doing. There are a couple of verbs here that are ours to do. For example, it's our job to *pray* and to *hear*. These two verbs go rather well together, since so much of praying is really listening. But most of the verbs are what we are praying for Jesus to do—*descend, cast out, enter in, be born, come, abide*. It can feel rude for us to be commanding the Lord of all Creation to do all these things. But maybe this is a way of letting him know that we are ready for him to do the

---

[16] Brooks, *United Methodist Hymnal*, 230.

things he has already done and has promised to do anyway.

The other words that stand out in this verse are the prepositions, the tiny little connecting words—come *to* us, abide *with* us, be born *in* us. To, with, and in. Advent is about all three of these words. It is about God in Christ coming to us, descending to us from the lofty throne in heaven to the little town of Bethlehem. It's about God in Christ coming to be with us, to abide with us, and to dwell with us as Emmanuel, "God with us." And it's about God in Christ wanting to be born in us, to live and grow in our own hearts and lives through the presence and power and peace of the Holy Spirit.

Today we light the fourth candle on our Advent wreath as a sign of our prayer that Christ's coming to us, his presence with us, and his life in us will be even more real for us this year than it has ever been, giving us the peace that only he can give.

A Vision for Peace in Bethlehem

Micah 5:2–5

But you, O Bethlehem of Ephrathah,
  who are one of the little clans of Judah,
from you shall come forth for me
  one who is to rule in Israel,
whose origin is from of old,
  from ancient days.
³ Therefore he shall give them up until the time
  when she who is in labor has brought forth;
then the rest of his kindred shall return
  to the people of Israel.
⁴ And he shall stand and feed his flock in the strength of
the Lord,
  in the majesty of the name of the Lord his God.
And they shall live secure, for now he shall be great
  to the ends of the earth,
⁵ and he shall be the one of peace.

In the Christmas story as we read it in Matthew, when the magi[17] arrived from the east, they first went to Jerusalem looking for the newborn king of the Jews (Matt 2:1). This makes sense because Jerusalem was the capital city. It was where the temple and the king's

---

[17] The Greek word for magi refers to astrologers, sorcerers, and magicians instead of kings.

palace were. But they didn't know exactly where to find him. So they asked for directions, which suggests that they may have been wise men after all, because wise people ask for directions!

But maybe it wasn't so wise for them to ask the sitting king where his successor had been born, especially a king as famously paranoid as Herod, who had his favorite wife, her mother, his brother-in-law, and three of his own sons executed in order to preserve his own reign.[18] Herod hadn't heard anything about a newborn king, so he asked the experts—the chief priests and the scribes, the religious leaders and scholars—where the Messiah was expected to be born. They readily responded that, according to the ancient prophet Micah, the Messiah was expected to be born in Bethlehem of Judea (Matt 2:5–6).

So, Herod sent the magi to go and search for the child, and when they had found him, to send word back to Herod, so that he might also go and worship him (although we can well imagine what kind of worship Herod has in mind). So they went to Bethlehem, following the star that had guided them thus far, until they found the place where the child was. They rejoiced as they entered the house where they found the child and his mother Mary (who apparently had upgraded

---

18 Hamilton, *Journey*, 123.

their accommodations from the manger stall), and they knelt down and worshiped him. They presented their precious gifts of gold, frankincense, and myrrh, and then they returned directly to their homeland, having been warned in a dream not to return to Herod (Matt 2:11–12).

Why Bethlehem?

This part of the Christmas story addresses a question that you may have had from the very beginning: Why Bethlehem? Why was Bethlehem the place where Jesus was born, and not Jerusalem, the capital city? Or Nazareth, where Jesus grew up? Or some other location?

The Gospel of Luke provides one answer to this question. Jesus was born in Bethlehem, according to Luke, because that was Joseph's hometown, and everyone had to return to their hometowns to be counted in the census the empire was conducting (Luke 2:3–4). Bethlehem, as we have already seen, was the home of the house and family of David, and Joseph was a descendant of David. So it's off to Bethlehem that he and Mary had to go. But Matthew gives us a different answer, a much more ancient answer, that goes all the way back seven hundred years to the time of the prophet Micah.

Micah was one of the so-called "minor" prophets, one of the twelve prophets in the Hebrew scriptures whose writings were shorter than the so-called "major" prophets like Isaiah, Jeremiah, and Ezekiel. He was also one of the early prophets, writing in the eighth century BCE. And he was one of the rural prophets who didn't come from the big city like Isaiah, but from the country, like his contemporary Amos.

Things are not well in Micah's world. It's not "peace on earth, good will to all." The world's a mess. Nothing is as it should be, as God intended it to be. There's insecurity and instability all around, both internally and internationally.

Internally, there's corruption throughout the land. The greedy rich are grabbing up land and property from the poor (2:1–2).[19] There's all sorts of cheating and scamming and changing the weights and measures in the business world (6:11). The judges and government officials are taking bribes (7:3). Even the preachers are in it for the money (3:11), and they're preaching only what the people want to hear (2:6, 11). There's all kinds of religious idolatry (5:13). Folks are just going through the motions, offering their sacrifices and burnt offerings, when what God most wants is for us "to do justice, and to love kindness, and to walk humbly with

---

[19] The parenthetical references in this paragraph are to the prophet Micah.

your God" (6:8). Instead, there's lying and deceit and violence in the streets (6:12). No one can trust anyone, not even friends and loved ones or lovers (7:5). Your enemies are those in your own home (7:6).

Internationally, the northern kingdom of Israel has been defeated and destroyed by the Assyrians, and Micah's own southern kingdom of Judah has only survived a similar fate so far because they've been paying off the Assyrians, who have nonetheless laid siege to Jerusalem. The first verse of the fifth chapter—the verse preceding the prophecy pertaining to Bethlehem—describes the city being surrounded by a wall and under siege, and the ruler (probably King Ahaz or Hezekiah) having been publicly humiliated by having to pay tribute to the Assyrians.

A New Hope

BUT, as the second verse of chapter five begins, all is not lost. There is yet hope. The prophet speaks of a new beginning to come from an unexpected place, the little town of Bethlehem. The prophet writes in words that evoke the ancient promise of God to David, the king who came from humble origins, the youngest of several sons, the shepherd boy:

But you, O Bethlehem of Ephrathah,
who are one of the little clans of Judah,
from you shall come forth for me one who is to rule in Israel,
whose origin is from of old, from ancient days. (Mic 5:2)

There may be pain and suffering for a time, but those in exile will return to their people, and this new leader will lead the people like a shepherd.

Therefore he shall give them up until the time
when she who is in labor has brought forth;
then the rest of his kindred shall return to the people of Israel.
And he shall stand and feed his flock in the strength of the Lord,
in the majesty of the name of the Lord his God. (Mic 5:3–4a)

The original identity of the woman in labor is unclear. Perhaps the prophet in his own time was referring specifically to the mother of the next king, possibly Hezekiah. Perhaps the prophet was suggesting generally that the time of this new beginning was at hand, as close as a woman in labor is to giving birth. Perhaps the prophet was speaking metaphorically of the nation as a woman in the labor pains of bringing new life and new hope to the people.

Ever since the birth of Jesus in Bethlehem, however, Christians can't help but hear this passage as ultimately referring to Mary, who arrived in Bethlehem in labor and brought forth the one whose origin, as Micah prophesies, is truly from of old, from ancient days (Mic 5:2). Indeed, according to the prologue of the Gospel of John, Christ's origin was from the very beginning. He was in fact the Word of God who was "in the beginning with God" and through whom "all things came into being . . . and without him not one thing came into being" (John 1:2–3).

And the hope was that this new leader to be born in Bethlehem would bring an end to the insecurity and instability that the people had been experiencing, both internally and internationally, and would bring to birth a time of peace and security. As the prophet continues:

And they shall live secure, for now he shall be great to the ends of the earth; and he shall be the one of peace. (Mic 5:4b–5a)

It is this last passage in particular that captures the longing of the people in and around Jerusalem and Bethlehem—in Micah's time, in Mary's time, and in modern times—for peace and security, to live with all the fullness of shalom.

This yearning for peace in all its fullness continues to resound amidst the ongoing conflicts between Israelis and Palestinians. But as Mitri Raheb, an author and pastor of the Christmas Lutheran Church in Bethlehem, has emphasized, this peace must come paired with justice for it to fully be peace. And it must be a justice, not just for one side or the other, but for all. A justice that is not justice for all is not justice at all. Our concern for justice for Israel, especially after the unconscionable attacks by Hamas in October 2023, must be balanced by a corresponding concern for justice for the Palestinians. "Without justice for the

Palestinians," Raheb has said, "there will not be peace for Israel. Justice is at the heart of the gospel. We cannot compromise on justice."[20]

But there has long been both a material as well as a mental and metaphorical wall preventing such a just peace from being realized in that conflicted place among these conflicted peoples.

Up Against a Wall

One of the major world historical events of my adolescence was the dissolution of the Soviet Union, or more properly, the Union of Soviet Socialist Republics (USSR). Though that dissolution formally occurred in late 1991, one of the primary precursors was a speech delivered by US President Ronald Reagan at the Brandenburg Gate in Berlin on June 12, 1987. In that speech, President Reagan referred to the famous "Berlin Wall" that separated Communist East Germany from the more capitalist West Germany as "part of a vast system of barriers that divides the entire continent of Europe." He went on to observe that "as long as this gate is closed, as long as this scar of a wall is permitted to stand, it is not the German question alone that remains open, but the question of freedom for all [humankind]." Reagan then posed his memorable challenge to his Russian counterpart

---

[20] Vioque, "Palestinian Christians," 15.

Mikhail Gorbachev: "If you seek peace, if you seek prosperity for the Soviet Union and Eastern Europe . . . Mr. Gorbachev, open this gate! Mr. Gorbachev, tear down this wall!"[21]

The Berlin wall is by no means the only wall that has ever been erected to separate peoples from one another. As already noted, Micah spoke in the verse immediately preceding the Bethlehem prophecy of the people being "walled around with a wall" and living under siege (Mic 5:1). There is even today a system of barriers, including walls, fences, and ditches, dating from the early 2000s that separates Jerusalem and Bethlehem, which is located in the Palestinian West Bank. For our tour group to enter into Bethlehem in 2014, we had to enter through a checkpoint at the security gate at the wall, with armed guards who could board our bus to check our credentials and approve our itineraries.

This wall, this separation barrier, has been quite controversial, not only among both Israelis and Palestinians, but also in the international community. Israel insists the barrier is necessary for greater security from Palestinian attacks, while Palestinians view the barrier as a symbol of occupation and racial segregation. Some compare it to the systemic

---

[21] Qtd in Robinson, "Tear Down."

separation of Whites and Blacks in apartheid South Africa. In addition to the wall, there is a ring of Israeli settlements surrounding Bethlehem, which essentially isolates Palestinians living in Bethlehem and its surrounding villages and contributes to a sense of their being under siege even today.

Regardless of what one thinks of the separation barriers in that area, it strikes me that the one whose birth we celebrate in Bethlehem was not at all about walls. In fact, he was all about tearing down walls of separation and division. Robert Frost's neighbor might have told him that "good fences make good neighbors," but the poet suspected that "something there is that doesn't love a wall, / That wants it down."[22] Jesus knew what that something was. He wanted the walls that divide us to come down, and he worked at building bridges between people instead.

Jesus As A Wall-Breaker

During his ministry, Jesus didn't just preach and teach and heal among his own people. He infuriated his hometown synagogue for suggesting that he would minister among Gentiles, outsiders, and foreigners, just like the prophets Elijah and Elisha long before him had done (Luke 4:16–30). True to his word, he healed the daughter of a Gentile woman (Matt 15:21–28, Mark

---

[22] Frost, "Mending Wall."

7:24–30). He taught his disciples to love not only those who can love you in return, but to also love your enemies and to pray for your persecutors (Matt 5:43–44, Luke 6:27–28). He practiced what he preached in his ministry with the Jews' ancient enemy the Samaritans when he revealed his identity as the Messiah for the first time to a Samaritan woman he met at a well (John 4:1–26), when he healed a Samaritan leper (Luke 17:11–19), and when he made a Samaritan the hero of one of his most famous stories (Luke 10:30–37). He called children to come to him, even though that was deemed improper for a teacher of his standing (Matt 18:13–15). He also healed the children and servants of the occupying government officials and military commanders.

Jesus ministered to men and women, young and old, rich and poor, Jew and Gentile. Jesus broke down all kinds of barriers and built all kinds of bridges throughout his ministry. He even broke down the ultimate barrier that existed between God and humanity when, at his death on the cross, the curtain of the temple that separated the most sacred area, the Holy of Holies, was torn in two, from top to bottom (Matt 27:51). Now, through Jesus, humanity could have direct and unmediated access to the presence of God.

The Apostle Paul addresses this barrier-breaking ministry of Jesus in his letter to the Ephesians where he describes how Gentiles, non-Jews, were once separated, cut off, kept apart from the promises of God, "having no hope and without God in the world" (Eph 2:12). But there is yet hope even for the Gentiles:

But now in Christ Jesus you who were once far off have been brought near by the blood of Christ. For he is our peace; in his flesh he has made both groups into one and has broken down the dividing wall, that is, the hostility between us . . . that he might create in himself one new humanity in place of the two, thus making peace. (Eph 2:13–15)

The wall that Paul likely had in mind here was the wall in the temple in Jerusalem that separated the Court of the Gentiles from the Court of Israel. Jesus brought about this peace and reconciliation, and he broke down this dividing wall that separated the Jews from the Gentiles in the temple, in the very same way and through the very same means as the curtain that separated humanity from God was torn in two. It was not through the sword—this new ruler of which Micah spoke would not be a warrior king like David was. He would not bring the longed-for peace and security to the people through force or power or might, but rather, as it turned out, in the unlikeliest of ways—through voluntarily submitting to force and power and might at the cross.

As Paul goes on to claim, Jesus "[reconciled] both groups to God in one body *through the cross*, thus putting to death that hostility through it" (Eph 2:16, emphasis added). It is at the cross that the material and metaphorical walls that separate and divide us from God and from one another fall away. It is the vertical arms of the cross that reconciles us to God, and it is the horizontal arms of the cross that reconciles us to one another, Jews and Gentiles. And so it is, Paul concludes, that Jesus "came and proclaimed peace to you who were far off and peace to those who were near; for through him both of us have access in one Spirit to the Father" (Eph 2:17–18).

It may seem odd and unexpected that it is through the cross that Jesus accomplished this peace and security for God's people, until we recall the shepherd imagery that Micah said would characterize this new ruler. "He shall stand and feed his flock in the strength of the Lord" (Mic 5:4). The new ruler would be a shepherd king, like David was. We recall how Jesus referred to himself as the Good Shepherd, and how he said, "the good shepherd lays down his life for the sheep" (John 10:11). Jesus was talking here about the cross, and also about his resurrection. "For this reason the Father loves me, because I lay down my life in order to take it up again" (John 10:17).

It is through both the cross and the empty tomb—through Jesus' death and resurrection—that Jesus the Good Shepherd would "stand and feed his flock in the strength of the Lord, in the majesty of the name of the Lord his God" (Mic 5:4). And it is through the cross and the empty tomb—through Jesus' death and resurrection—that he has brought to birth a very different kind of peace and security than the people, both then and now, might have wanted. But in the end, it's the kind of peace and security that ultimately matters—the peace of the pardon of our sins and the security of our eternal salvation. "Pardon for sin and a peace that endureth," as we sing in an old familiar hymn.[23] It's a peace, as Jesus says, not as the world gives, but that only he can give us. Therefore, "do not let your hearts be troubled, and do not let them be afraid" (John 14:27).

The Last Word

This is the good news of Christmas, the coming of the one who can truly save us from our sins and offer us the peace and security for which we most deeply yearn. And it is the good news that the prophet Micah points to, not only in the Bethlehem prophecy, but in his closing words. I love how the book of Micah ends:

---

[23] Chisholm, *United Methodist Hymnal*, 140.

Who is a God like you,[24] *pardoning iniquity*
and passing over the transgression
of the remnant of your possession?
He does not retain his anger forever,
because he delights in showing clemency.
He will again have compassion upon us;
he will tread our iniquities under foot. (Mic 7:18–19a)

Then the prophet shifts from talking about God and God's grace to talking to God in a spirit of praise and thanksgiving:

You will cast all our sins
into the depths of the sea.
You will show faithfulness to Jacob
and unswerving loyalty to Abraham,
as you have sworn to our ancestors
from the days of old. (Mic 7:19b–20)

These are the last words of the prophet Micah. The last word is grace. Contrary to many popular misrepresentations, the Old Testament is not all judgment. The prophets are not all doom and gloom. There is such great grace throughout the Bible. It threads through the entirety of the scriptures. The love and compassion and mercy of God resounds

---

[24] This is a play on the name of Micah, which means "who is like the Lord?"

throughout the Hebrew scriptures as well as through the New Testament. Because, after all, it is the same God, the Lord of all creation, who is the one who became flesh, who took on human form and dwelt among us in the baby born—just like the prophet long ago said—in Bethlehem.

Questions for Refection and Discussion

1. What are some walls that you see in your congregation, in your community, in our country and in our world, or in your life today?

2. Where might some walls or borders or boundaries be appropriate or even necessary?

3. What walls do you think Jesus would want to tear down today?

4. How might your church or congregation be called to be a wall breaker and a bridge builder in your community? What in particular might you be able to contribute to these efforts?

5. The Hebrew word for peace, *shalom*, means not just the absence of war and violence but more fully the presence of justice and wellness and wholeness for both individuals and communities. Where do you see a longing for the fullness of *shalom* in the world, in your community, in your own life? How can Jesus' life and ministry answer this longing?

Christmas Eve

Christ

Where children pure and happy pray to the bless-ed Child,
Where misery cries out to Thee, Son of the mother mild;
Where charity stands watching and faith holds wide the door;
The dark night wakes, the glory breaks, and Christmas comes
once more.

This verse is not included in our hymnals, but it is one of the verses that the Rev. Phillips Brooks originally wrote for the beloved carol "O Little Town of Bethlehem." Though it was composed for the children's Christmas program, this is the only verse that explicitly mentions children.

Its juxtaposition of a picture of innocent children sweetly praying to Jesus with people in misery crying out to Christ is jarring, but it recalls the restless misery that was in the world when Jesus was born and is still in the world today, especially in places like Ukraine, Gaza, and the land of Jesus' birth. And it is so often the innocent ones, the children, who suffer the most.

Yet the hymn does not leave us without hope. It pictures charity—whose other name is love—standing watch like a sentinel, and faith with its arms out wide holding open the door for the one for whom we've been waiting to enter in. And sure enough, the new day dawns, dispelling the darkness, and once again it's Christmas.

And so we light the candle in the center of our Advent wreath, the Christ candle, as we celebrate the birth of the one who is the very center of our lives, the life of our church, and the life of the world. "What has come into being in him," the Gospel of John tells us, "was life, and the life was the light of all people" (John 1:4). On Christmas Eve, we rejoice that "the light (of Christ) shines in the darkness, and the darkness did not overcome it" (John 1:5).

Let Us Go Now to Bethlehem

Luke 2:1–20

In those days a decree went out from Caesar Augustus that all the world should be registered. ²This was the first registration and was taken while Quirinius was governor of Syria. ³All went to their own towns to be registered. ⁴Joseph also went from the town of Nazareth in Galilee to Judea, to the city of David called Bethlehem, because he was descended from the house and family of David. ⁵He went to be registered with Mary, to whom he was engaged and who was expecting a child. ⁶While they were there, the time came for her to deliver her child. ⁷And she gave birth to her firstborn son and wrapped him in bands of cloth and laid him in a manger, because there was no place in the guest room.

⁸Now in that same region there were shepherds living in the fields, keeping watch over their flock by night. ⁹Then an angel of the Lord stood before them, and the glory of the Lord shone around them, and they were terrified. ¹⁰But the angel said to them, "Do not be afraid, for see, I am bringing you good news of great joy for all the people: ¹¹to you is born this day in the city of David a Savior, who is the Messiah, the Lord. ¹²This will be a sign for you: you will find a child wrapped in bands of cloth and lying in a manger." ¹³And suddenly there was with the angel a multitude of the heavenly host, praising God and saying,

¹⁴"Glory to God in the highest heaven, and on earth peace among those whom he favors!"

[15] When the angels had left them and gone into heaven, the shepherds said to one another, "Let us go now to Bethlehem and see this thing that has taken place, which the Lord has made known to us." [16] So they went with haste and found Mary and Joseph and the child lying in the manger. [17] When they saw this, they made known what had been told them about this child, [18] and all who heard it were amazed at what the shepherds told them, [19] and Mary treasured all these words and pondered them in her heart. [20] The shepherds returned, glorifying and praising God for all they had heard and seen, just as it had been told them.

Christmas Eve in Bethlehem is normally quite the festive place to be. There's usually a giant Christmas tree set up in Manger Square, just outside of the Church of the Nativity, around which both locals and pilgrims from all over the world gather to sing Christmas carols and celebrate the birth of Jesus. The streets are lined with booths and bazaars where artisans sell handmade gifts and ornaments. But after the Israel-Hamas war broke out in October 2023, Christmas Eve in Bethlehem was very different. The customary celebrations, which annually attract thousands of Christians, were canceled. The city's mayor said that the joyous festivities were out of the question with so much violence and suffering taking place. Church leaders still planned to gather together, however, for Midnight Mass and to pray for peace in the place where the Prince of Peace was born.

Not only was Christmas in Bethlehem canceled that December because of the Israel-Hamas war, but a trip to the Holy Land that some members of my congregation had planned also had to be postponed. They were to have left two weeks after the war began. We have all been praying with all the people in the Holy Land and all around the world for justice and peace in that place where Jesus was born. But until that time comes, and until pilgrims can travel safely again to Bethlehem, I invite you to travel there in your imagination—to hear, and to heed, the invitation of the shepherds in the Christmas story: "Let us go now to Bethlehem and see this thing that has taken place, which the Lord has made known to us" (Luke 2:15).

A Church of Contrasts

When my wife Tracy and I had the opportunity to travel to the Holy Land in the spring of 2014 with some members of our church at the time, we, of course, went to Bethlehem. As we were making our way in our motorcoach through the city, I saw lots of shops and street vendors that signaled that tourism is indeed their main industry. I especially remember seeing a familiar looking green and white sign above a coffee shop. Then I looked more closely and saw that it read "Stars & Bucks." How clever! I believe it was our tour guide who suggested their motto is "you see the stars, you pay the bucks!"

Soon we arrived at the Church of the Nativity, the oldest standing church in the Holy Land. It was one of the churches that the Emperor Constantine's mother Queen Helena wanted to have been built after she toured the area. It was commissioned in the year 326 and consecrated in 339. It's built over the cave or grotto that is believed to have been the actual site of the animal stable where Jesus was born. It's been built up, added onto, damaged, repaired (scaffolding was up when we visited there), and preserved over the years. Some of the original mosaic tile flooring is still visible in some places. Persian invaders allegedly spared the church from destruction in the seventh century because the Magi depicted in the mosaics looked like Persians!

The odd thing about this church, however, is that from the outside, it doesn't necessarily look like a church, at least not like the kinds of churches with which I am most familiar. The church doesn't stand out, but instead it seems to blend in with all the surrounding sandstone buildings. There are a couple of short steeples on the corners that have crosses on the tops that identify it as a church, but they are rather understated. The overall appearance is relatively non-descript, especially compared to some of the other iconic churches in Christendom that I've visited, such as Notre Dame in Paris, Westminster Abbey in London, and the National Cathedral in Washington,

DC, with their soaring belltowers and brilliant stained-glass windows.

These iconic churches also have grand and unmistakable entrances, adorned with carvings of saints and other Christian symbols. But if you didn't know where to look, you would probably miss the entrance to the Church of the Nativity, which is a simple, low door only about five feet high. You can see the outline of a much larger entrance above and around it, and then a smaller arch from the times of the Crusades. But the current entrance is this tiny door.

The church's entrance was reportedly downsized during the Ottoman period to keep merchants and marauders from riding their horses and bringing their carts into the church. Now the door is called the "Door of Humility." Most people have to kneel or duck down to enter through it. Tracy went ahead of me and snapped a photo of me coming through the door.

But once you are inside the church, it's a different story. If the outside appearance is very simple and humble, the interior is quite ornate, even opulent. There are bright frescoes on the walls, brass lanterns hanging from the ceiling, gold and silver screens separating the chancel, and the smell of incense burning in the side chapels. It seems that the nations have been bringing gold, frankincense, and more to the birthplace of Jesus for centuries! The contrast between the understated exterior and elaborate interior is probably the most pronounced of any church I've ever visited.

I remember feeling a bit put off at first by the extreme contrast between the humble entry to the church and the ornate interior of it. It felt a bit like aesthetic whiplash. I thought all the gold and silver and brass inside was a tad gaudy and a bit busy. It certainly wasn't the first time I had been inside a sanctuary that I thought was more showy than Jesus would have liked. But upon reflection, I've come to wonder if the Church of the Nativity might be something of a metaphor of the Christian life itself.

The only entry to the life of Christian discipleship is by way of the door of humility. Contrary to popular misperceptions, humility is not thinking less highly of ourselves than we ought to, but rather thinking more rightly of ourselves. It's seeing ourselves for who we are. It involves freely and honestly admitting our need to be saved—saved from our sin, from our selfishness and self-centeredness, and from our warped relationships with God, with others, and with ourselves. It means acknowledging that we cannot save ourselves. We cannot extricate ourselves from the messes in which we find ourselves, both of our own making and otherwise. We need help. We need God's help. We need divine assistance. We need, in other words, grace.

But once we enter into this humble awareness both of our need for God's grace and the availability of it to us and to all people in Jesus Christ, the extravagant riches of God's grace open up to us and are poured out upon us by the Holy Spirit. The glory of God in which we were originally created, that had been tarnished and clouded over by our sin, gradually becomes polished by God's transforming grace, and we start to shimmer and shine in newness of life. I remember learning from polishing my mom's silver that well-polished silver reflects the image of the beholder. That's what God's grace does in us. It polishes us until we reflect more and more fully the image of the one who beholds us in Christ Jesus. So in that way, the Christian life is like the Church of the Nativity—you enter by way of humility, and then you are led by God's polishing, sanctifying grace into the greater glory of God's majesty.

A Melody at the Manger

While we were inside the church, we stood in a line that wove in and out of the pillars that were in the process of being renovated. We waited for over two hours. Our guide told us we were lucky that day because the line is often out the door and into Manger Square. We were waiting to go down a steep set of stairs to the area underneath the main level of the church where the cave or the grotto where Jesus is believed to have been born is located.

This is unlike any cave I've ever been in. In the center is something like a fireplace, enclosed with bright red curtains, with brass lanterns hanging inside. On the floor, there is a fourteen-point silver star that marks the traditional site of the manger. The fourteen points recall the triple cycle of fourteen generations that the Gospel of Matthew traces from Abraham to Jesus (Matt 1:1–17). Each of us waited for our turn to kneel down, touch the star, whisper a brief prayer, and then make our way back up the staircase on the opposite side. Tracy was behind me, and she took a photo of me touching the star. I didn't realize I had my own personal photographer!

If I'm being honest, I was a bit underwhelmed by the experience. I was having a hard time sensing the sacredness of the site when it felt like we were being herded through like sheep. But our shepherd, our tour guide, gathered his flock together in a side room just off the main area of the cave, out of the flow of traffic. All of us in the group were bunched in together there, over forty of us. Before we went back upstairs, he didn't want us to miss the significance of where we were and what had taken place there.

He asked us what song we most associate with the Christmas story. The quick consensus was "Silent Night." So we began to sing together the first verse of "Silent Night" in that side room. Tracy got a little teary-eyed because she remembered her mom used to sing that song to her when she was a child as a lullaby. In the midst of all the crowds around us, "all is calm." In the midst of the darkness in that chapel and around the world, "all is bright." I believe that's when it sank in, at least for me, where we were and what it was really all about. "Christ the Savior is born, Christ the Savior is born."

That is what Christmas Eve is all about. That's why this evening is so special, so significant.

Bethlehem Is Here

Perhaps you have spent a lot of time this season waiting in long lines yourself. Perhaps at a store. Perhaps at the airport. Perhaps even at church.

Perhaps you find yourself and those you love caught, on the one hand, between the exorbitance and the extravagance and the excessiveness that seems to be expected of us this time of year, and on the other hand, the simplicity and the humility that the Christmas story invites of us every year.

Perhaps on this night you find yourself trying your best to honor the traditions of those who have gone before you while also just yearning to sneak in a quiet moment of silence and worship and prayer amidst all the hustle and bustle.

Let me let you in on a little secret. Or maybe just remind you of something you probably already know but is sometimes easy to forget.

This is the Door of Humility.

Wherever you may find yourself, this is the side room.

This is the place where you can come and remember what this night is all about.

And you don't have to travel halfway around the world. Bethlehem is right here.

Bethlehem. "The house of bread."

The bread of heaven is here. Jesus Christ is here with us in bread and cup.

And all are welcome. All are invited to the manger of the Messiah.

So come. "Let us go now to Bethlehem and see this thing that has taken place, that the Lord has made known to us."

Invitation to Break Bread in Bethlehem

Instead of inviting you to consider questions for personal reflection and group discussion following this final chapter, I would like to invite you to mark the completion of this Advent journey by breaking bread with family members, friends, fellow study participants, or your faith community in honor of the "house of bread" that is Bethlehem. Here are three options for you to consider.

First, many congregations that gather for worship on Christmas Eve and/or Christmas Day include the celebration of the sacrament of Holy Communion in their services. Could there be a more appropriate way for us to celebrate the advent of the Word of God become flesh and abiding among us in Christ Jesus than by sharing in the bread and the cup of his flesh and blood? While the mood of this sacrament might be mournful on a day like Maundy Thursday, on Christmas Eve the mood is more mystical. The words from the fourth-century liturgy of St. James that became the hymn "Let All Mortal Flesh Keep Silence" capture the mood well:

King of kings, yet born of Mary, as of old on earth he stood,
Lord of Lords, in human vesture, in the body and the blood;
he will give to all the faithful his own self for heavenly food.[25]

---

[25] Moultrie, "Let All Mortal Flesh Keep Silence," st. 2.

And as we share in the sacrament in our own churches, we are also joining together in spirit with Christians all around the world, from Bethlehem, Palestine, to Bethlehem, Pennsylvania, from all different nations and denominations, at the table of the Lord. Perhaps we Christians most closely approximate the spirit of unity in Christ for which he prayed in John 17 when we gather together for Christmas Communion.

Second, a Love Feast is a fellowship meal that recalls the meals that Jesus regularly enjoyed with his disciples and others throughout the Gospels and that the early church carried forward in their gatherings (Acts 2:46). The tradition of the Love Feast came into Methodist practice through the influence of the Moravians (Lutheran Pietists) whom John Wesley encountered in Savannah, Georgia, in 1737. In his diary, he wrote, "After evening prayers, we joined with the Germans in one of their love-feasts. It was begun and ended with thanksgiving and prayer, and celebrated in so decent and solemn a manner as a Christian of the apostolic age would have allowed to be worthy of Christ."[26]

A Love Feast is different from the sacrament of Holy Communion. It does not require a licensed or ordained minister to preside; any Christian can lead one. It is often held in more informal settings like homes,

---

[26] United Methodist Church, "Love Feast," 581.

fellowship halls, or small group classrooms. Love Feasts ideally include prayers of thanksgiving, songs of praise, readings of scripture, and words of testimony where participants share how they have experienced and encountered God's presence, guidance, and peace. A loaf of bread, perhaps baked especially for this occasion, is broken and passed among participants, along with (customarily) water or other simple beverages to drink (care is taken that the elements of the Love Feast won't be confused with Communion bread and wine or grape juice). A fuller fellowship meal can also accompany the Love Feast.

A celebration of a Love Feast with a small group at the conclusion of this study could include a time of singing some of the carols of the season, reading together the stories of Christ's birth from Matthew 2 and Luke 2, praying with and for one another and for the people of the world into which Christ has come, sharing testimonies of how your faith has been impacted through participating in this study, and perhaps even collecting an offering to share with a community ministry or a particular situation of need or concern.

For more information on how you might celebrate a Love Feast in your context, visit:

https://www.umc.org/en/content/methodist-history-the-what-and-why-of-love-feasts.

A third option might be simply to recognize and rejoice in the presence of the Christ of Christmas with you and your friends and family as you gather around the table to break bread, wherever it is that table may be and whomever it is may be seated at it. You might share with one another how you have experienced Christ's presence with you that year, or how you are praying for Christ's presence to become more real in your life, in your church, or in the world.

And just as the risen Jesus was welcomed as a stranger at a table in Emmaus and was then recognized in the breaking of bread, so too might our holiday tables be ideal places to invite strangers or others to join us (Luke 24:28–35). Are there persons you know who may find themselves alone this Christmas, without family members close by or who will be coming to visit them? Consider residents in nursing homes or assisted living communities; students at the local college or university who can't go home for the holidays; persons whose loved ones are hospitalized, incarcerated, or serving abroad in the military; persons who have been separated or divorced; those who have lost a spouse, or a parent, or a child, or even a beloved pet. We just might experience the presence of Christ with us through them, and they might experience the presence of Christ through us.

Every house can be a house of bread when Jesus is there. Every table can be Bethlehem. As Jesus said, "where two or three are gathered in my name, I am there among them" (Matt 18:20).

Bibliography

Blincoe, Nicholas. *Bethlehem: Biography of a Town.* London: Constable, 2017.

Brooks, Phillips. "O Little Town of Bethlehem." In *The United Methodist Hymnal*, hymn 230. Nashville: United Methodist Publishing House, 1989.

Chisholm, Thomas O. "Great Is Thy Faithfulness." In *The United Methodist Hymnal*, hymn 140. Nashville: United Methodist Publishing House, 1989.

Hamilton, Adam. *The Journey: Walking the Road to Bethlehem.* Nashville: Abingdon, 2011.

Kolin, Philip. "Eliab's complaint." *Christian Century.* December 24, 2014. https://www.christiancentury.org/artsculture/poems/eliab-s-complaint

Morgan, Robert J. *Then Sings My Soul: 150 of the World's Greatest Hymn Stories.* Nashville: Thomas Nelson, 2003.

Morse, Christopher. *Not Every Spirit: A Dogmatics of Christian Disbelief.* Valley Forge, PA: Trinity, 1994.

Moultrie, Gerald, trans. "Let All Mortal Flesh Keep Silence." In *The United Methodist Hymnal*, hymn 626. Nashville: United Methodist Publishing House, 1989.

Osbeck, Kenneth W. *101 Hymn Stories: The Inspiring True Stories Behind 101 Favorite Hymns.* Grand Rapids, MI: Kregel, 1982.

Robinson, Peter. "Tear Down This Wall." *National Archives Prologue.* Summer 2007.

https://www.archives.gov/publications/prologue/2007/summer/berlin.html

United Methodist Church. "The Love Feast." In *The United Methodist Book of Worship*, 581–582. Nashville: United Methodist Publishing House, 1992.

Villegas, Israel S. "Tear gas over the soccer field." *Christian Century.* June 2024.

Vioque, Hanna. "Palestinian Christians hear empty words in Western churches' calls for cease-fire." *Christian Century.* March 2024.

Wolpe, David. *David: The Divided Heart.* Yale, 2014.